THE FOUR GOSPELS

THE FOUR GOSPELS
AN INTRODUCTION

HUBERT RICHARDS

McCRIMMONS
Great Wakering, Essex, United Kingdom

This book is for Clare, Pedro and Blanca.

ACKNOWLEDGEMENTS

Cardinal Cormac Murphy-O'Connor for his continued support for my work.

My wife Clare for putting my writing into digital form, and for her patience in dealing with countless snags.

Teresa McLaughlin for her support and zealous correcting of many of my mistakes.

All who have helped to make this book better than it would have been if left only to me.

First published in 2007 in the United Kingdom by
MCCRIMMON PUBLISHING CO. LTD.
10-12 High Street, Great Wakering, Essex SS3 0EQ
E-mail: info@mccrimmons.com / Web: www.mccrimmons.com

Text © 2007 Hubert J. Richards

ISBN 978-085597-689-7

Typeset in Zapf International Light 11/14pt
Text printed on 100gsm offset / Cover printed on 260gsm art
Printed and bound by Thanet Press Ltd., Margate, Kent, UK

Contents

Foreword

THE TITLE GIVEN TO A BOOK tells you a good deal about the way it should be read. If it includes the word 'history' or 'chronicle' or 'biography', then you would expect to read a straightforward factual and accurate account of the historical period or person under discussion. Obviously a certain amount of interpretation would be required: nobody wants to read a simple shopping list of facts. But such interpretation would be as fair and tentative and unbiased as possible.

The early Christians were familiar with history books: there were plenty about. Three hundred years earlier Xenophon had written a life of Socrates, and called it *Memoirs*. At the same time as Matthew, Mark and Luke were at work, Plutarch was writing his account of famous Romans and called it *Lives*. A little later, Tacitus wrote two accounts of the events he had lived through, and called one of them *History* and the other *Annals*.

The first century Christians who published the writings of Matthew, Mark, Luke and John could have used any of these familiar titles. They didn't. They chose the title of 'Gospel'. The Anglo-Saxon word means 'good news', and is an exact translation of the Greek word given to these writings by the early Christians: *evangelion*. They were aware that these pieces were not a mere chronicle or history of events. They were proclamations of good news. They were written not to inform people about Christianity, but to invite them to join, not to give them 'the gen', but to bring them joy, not to retail a history, but to proclaim a mystery. The Gospels, in short, are openly presented as preaching, in other words as Christian propaganda.

The word 'propaganda' may jar on some ears. But what other word should one use for pieces which are designed to propagate a particular point of view? The Gospels are not unbiased news reports: their aim is to convert the reader.

Not by bending the facts. They are demonstrably built around the public life and teaching of Jesus: witness the detailed description of his trial and death. But the emphasis is never on when and where and why and in what circumstances Jesus preached his good news. Such details remain secondary to the extraordinary impact his teaching had on all and sundry, on sympathisers and opponents, on friends and foes alike. The authors are not trying to provide us with neutral information. They are offering four theologies, the proclamation of the Good News, presented from four different angles, according to Matthew, according to Mark, according to Luke and according to John. However, they are putting the same loaded question: 'Do you see this as good news? If so, come and join us'.

Symbols of the Gospel writers

THE FOUR GOSPEL WRITERS have traditionally been represented by four symbolic figures – a lion, an ox, a man and an eagle. Why?

Originally these four were all combined in a single sphinx-like creature with a lion's body, a man's head, an ox's legs and an eagle's wings.

Forbidding figures in this style (called *karibu* or *cherubim*) guarded the palaces and temples of the ancient East, as much as to say 'Royal Enclosure'.

It was the last book of the Bible that eventually turned these four characteristics into four separate creatures, with one characteristic each.

'The first...was like a lion...
the second like a bull...
the third...had a human face...and
the fourth... was like a flying eagle.'

Revelation 4:7

The figures of the lion, bull, man and eagle, suggest all that is noblest, strongest, wisest, most swift, in the created world. Since the time of Irenaeus, these four creatures have been used as symbols of the four Gospel writers, perhaps because they vaguely fitted their opening lines:

Mark (a lion roaring in the desert),
Matthew (a human genealogy),
Luke (the Temple with its animal sacrifices),
John (a bird's-eye view of the whole).

The Gospel of
MARK

The Gospel of Mark

Don't imagine it will be an easy ride!

WE BEGIN WITH THE GOSPEL OF MARK. The large majority of scholars agree that, in the form the four Gospels have come down to us, this was the first to be written.

You need to read a piece of Mark's Gospel in close parallel with the other Gospels, and compare each line word by word, in order to realise what a brilliant writer he is. Take the story of Jesus and the children, for instance. Here is a literal translation of the original:

Mark 10	Matthew 19	Luke 18
13	**13**	**15**
And people were bringing children to him for him to touch them	Then people brought children to him for him to lay hands on them and pray.	People were even bringing babies to him for him to touch them.
		Having seen this
But the disciples scolded them.	But the disciples scolded them.	the disciples began to scold them.
14	**14**	**16**
But Jesus *having seen this was dismayed*	But Jesus	But Jesus
		called (the children) saying,
and said to them, Let the children	said to them, Let the children (alone) and do not stop them	Let the children
come to me. Do not stop them, because the Kingdom of God is (made) of such as these.	coming to me. because the Kingdom of Heaven is (made) of such as these.	come to me, and do not stop them, because the Kingdom of God is (made) of such as these.

Mark 10	Matthew 19	Luke 18
15 In truth I tell you, whoever does not welcome the Kingdom of God like a child will not enter it.		**17** In truth I tell you, whoever does not welcome the Kingdom of God like a child will not enter it.
16 *And having embraced them,* *he blesses* (them) having placed his hands on them.	**15** And having placed his hands on them, he went his way.	

No one can fail to notice Mark's touch here. He alone mentions Jesus' awareness, Jesus' dismay, Jesus embracing the children, and Jesus pronouncing a blessing on them. Matthew and Luke wrote their Gospels with a copy of Mark in front of them, but chose to leave those phrases out. Their Gospels are never as vivid as Mark's.

MARK'S STYLE

It is the same in story after story. If you want the feeling of actually being present at the scene, of hearing the actual words spoken by Jesus in the original Aramaic – *Ephphatha* (7:34), *Talitha kum* (5:41), *Abba* (14:36) – go to Mark.

If you like hearing stories told in the disjointed, disorderly and repetitious style of the man in the street, with the past tense easily slipping into the present ('He left there and went to the next village, and this man comes up and says …') go to Mark. He uses this 'historic present tense', as in the excerpt above, 150 times. Luke will cut out 140 of them. Modern translations cut all of them.

If you enjoy the sort of detail which is quite irrelevant to the story but brings it to life – the cushion in the stern of the boat (4:38), the crowds sitting down on the hillside, literally 'like flowerbeds on the green grass' (6:39), the whiteness of the transfiguration 'such as no washing powder could give you' (9:3) – go to Mark.

You almost need to read Mark in an accent or dialect to get the flavour. Matthew and Luke, when they followed him, found him far too blunt and colloquial to copy word for word. Their own versions of the Gospel (not to mention of Jesus and the disciples) are far more polished and sophisticated.

Translators who put Mark into English hardly dare to give an exact and literal rendering of what he wrote: it wouldn't read like a piece of literature. But in the original Greek, Mark's Gospel is a very rough diamond indeed. His very first chapter uses the word 'and' 75 times within the span of 40 verses, most often at the beginning of a sentence.

With his unfinished sentences and breathless pace (he uses the word 'immediately' 42 times; Luke reduces these to seven), Mark presents a vivid and haphazard succession of scenes from the life of Jesus. They are thrown up at the reader like series of images in a pop-video. There is little of Jesus' preaching – that all comes in the other three gospels. For Mark, Jesus' preaching lies in what he *is* and what he *does*.

A BIOGRAPHY?

This must sound as if Mark's main purpose in writing was to provide a biography, and that he was concerned to keep an exact record of the events in the life of Jesus, before people began to put their own interpretation on events.

But this would be to underrate him. Mark interprets Jesus quite as boldly as the other Gospel-writers do. He says so in his opening lines: 'Here begins the Good News about Jesus the Messiah-Christ, the *Son of God*'. What could it possibly mean to be Son of God? Mark wrote his Gospel to try to spell out an answer.

Notice that this title 'Son of God', which crops up frequently enough throughout the pages of Matthew and Luke (not to mention John), is in this Gospel not given again to Jesus until the last page. Voices from heaven and voices from hell proclaim him Son of God, but no human being does so until Jesus is hanging on the cross, only sixteen verses before the end of the story (15:39). According to Mark, you have to wait till then before you really understand what that title means.

MYSTERY

Is there some mystery about the title, then, that makes it difficult to understand? Of course there is!

Mark underlines the mystery by having people ask, again and again, from page one on, 'Who is this?' When Jesus speaks, people are constantly bowled over, saying they've never heard the like. When Jesus heals people, particularly of psychiatric sickness, everyone keeps saying, 'We've never seen this sort of thing before'.

Jesus is regularly misunderstood in this Gospel, even nineteen times by his own disciples. Everyone keeps being seized with fear in his presence (27 times). Most strangely of all, the Jesus of Mark's Gospel keeps telling people not to reveal who he is. The phrase comes up so many times that Matthew and Luke, when they copied Mark, found it far too prominent, and cut it down severely.

But Mark insists that you musn't come to a conclusion about Jesus too quickly. There is a mystery about him. He is an enigma, a puzzle that can't be solved glibly. Why?

A GOSPEL FOR THE PERSECUTED

Mark's Gospel was probably written in Rome, about 65 to 70AD. They were years of turmoil, with Rome burnt down in the year 64, Peter crucified in 65 and Paul beheaded in 67, Nero committing suicide in 68, and four rival generals fighting over the empty throne.

These were years in which the small community of Christians in Rome were viciously persecuted by Nero's police. Many of them were martyred. Their friends and relatives must have wondered whether there was any point in proclaiming Jesus as Son of God if it only got you a good hiding!

Mark wrote his Gospel to explain to the Christians of Rome that, in the kind of world we live in, no one can be a son of God without getting a good hiding, Jesus first and then his followers. Jesus' suffering and death were not some unfortunate accident which could have been avoided. They were the very meaning of his life. He was Son of God, not in spite of his death, but because of it. If he had not suffered and died, it would have proved he was not Son of God.

DO YOU UNDERSTAND?

This means that until you reach the final pages that tell of his suffering, you haven't really grasped who he is. You'll have your own expectations about what a Son of God should be like, and you'll give Jesus that title because of his attractive teaching, or his marvellous healing powers, not imagining that these will get him into trouble.

But that would be such a misunderstanding of what being Son of God involves that Jesus would repudiate you, as he did Peter, with the fierce words, 'Get behind me, Satan!' (8:33)

You cannot yet tell who Jesus really is. You must not call him Son of God till you get to the cross. That's where you'll finally really understand what being a son of God is all about. Whether you live in Jerusalem or Rome, in Newcastle or New York. So be warned, because even his closest friends can get it wrong.

FIRST CHRISTIAN DRAMATIST

St Paul had already written his famous epistles to the churches when Mark sat down to write this Gospel. They contain a very similar interpretation of the meaning of Jesus' life and death. Listen to him writing to the Christians of Corinth about the year 57AD:

> We are surrounded by difficulties on all sides, but never crushed.
> We see no answer to our problems, but never despair.
> We are constantly persecuted, but never forsaken by God.
> We are forever being struck down, but never destroyed.
> Our bodies are carrying the death of Jesus wherever we go,
> but they also proclaim the fact that Jesus lives on.
> Our union with Jesus may condemn us to death day by day,
> but it also tells everyone how we are his living body.
>
> 2 Corinthians 4:8-11

The language Paul uses to make his point is that of theology. Mark has simply turned this theology into a narrative.

Matthew, Luke and John later found this formula so brilliant that they each adopted it, and like Mark presented the meaning of Jesus by means of stories. Christians have ample reason to be grateful to Mark the inventor, the First Christian Dramatist.

A FEW FOOTNOTES TO MARK'S GOSPEL

1:1 The Risen Son of God
Though he is more 'primitive' than Matthew, Luke or John, Mark is not less 'theological'. He is not writing a mere biography of Jesus. His opening line states that he believes him to be the Son of God. Notice, that the very first appearance of Jesus is told in resurrection terms (see v.10): he emerges from the waters of death to be declared Son of God, and to reveal that the heavens are now open and the Spirit of God made available to all.

1:39 The Kingdom of Satan
Within less than forty verses, Mark has already mentioned evil spirits eight times. He sees a world in the grip of Satan, and Jesus' ministry as a costly battle to liberate the human race from the forces of evil, and to re-establish the kingship of God.

2:27 Priorities
Jews kept (and still keep) the Saturday of each week as a 'holy day'. As a good Jew, Jesus respected this, as did his first followers (see *Acts of the Apostles* 1:12, 13:14ff, 16:13, 18:4). In spite of this, Jesus' remark here (and no one states it more clearly than Mark) is more radical than anything else he is reported to have said. Institutions and organisations, systems and governments, laws and rules, vaticans and canterburys, however sacred – these exist for people, not vice versa. No *status quo* is absolute or sacrosanct, only human beings.

4:12 Why parables?
Mark's explanation is fiercer than Matthew's. Jesus teaches in parables, not *because* his hearers are blind, but *in order* to make them blind! Mark sees the enigmatic parables as part of the mystery of Jesus. They will not make sense to the superficial, only to those who understand his mission, and are willing to share it.

6:5 Miracles
Matthew says that Jesus *did* not do any miracles in his hometown because of people's lack of faith. Mark more honestly says he *could* not. It is simply impossible to reveal the hand of God to minds that are closed.

8:29 Messiah-Christ
This is the first time since the opening line of Mark's Gospel that the title 'Messiah' (Christ) is given to Jesus. The question repeatedly asked in the previous chapters, 'Who is this man?' is here given the answer. For Mark, this forms the climax of his story. From here on, the enormous implications must be opened out.

9:32 They did not understand
Misunderstanding of Jesus' mission is prominent in these chapters: Peter's 'satanic' plan to avoid trouble in Jerusalem (8:32); the argument about leadership (9:34); the in-fighting about high rank (10:38). Mark is again stressing that what is entailed in being a son of God is so difficult to grasp, that even Jesus' closest friends got it wrong. People can't understand the Gospel till they live it.

11:9 Hosanna
The words 'Blessed is he who comes' are so much part of the normal greeting given to pilgrims that they are still displayed outside Israeli cities today. On feast days in Jesus' time, all pilgrims were welcomed into Jerusalem, as Jesus is here, with palm branches known as 'hosannas'. The messianic overtones of the scene are elaborated in the other Gospels, but not in Mark.

12:43 The Widow's Mite
What an observant Jesus, who can see a parable in everything! The poor woman's last copper coin, given to the Temple Fund, is as prodigal as God himself, and as improvident as Jesus' own giving of his all on the cross, hardly likely to make any difference to the world.

14:1 The Passion Story

All the Gospels emphasise Jesus' passion and death as the climax of their stories. As Mark tells it, it occupies as much as a third of his Gospel: all the rest is no more than a long prologue. Here the 'secret' is finally unveiled.

15:33 Godforsaken

How can anyone feel so utterly abandoned by God, and be recognised at that moment as the very Son of God? Mark leaves it to the reader to understand.

16:8 Silence

Most Bibles point out in a footnote that the oldest manuscripts of Mark's Gospel end here. The 'longer ending' is a stringing together of extracts from Matthew, Luke and John. Mark himself seems to have wanted to end his Gospel with the observation that anyone else who had finally seen its meaning would be as bewildered and awestruck as these women disciples of Jesus, and silent.

The Gospel of
MATTHEW

The Gospel of Matthew

Matthew's Jesus is pre-eminently The Teacher

SOMEONE WITH NOTHING BETTER TO DO once worked out that the Hebrew Bible has exactly 1068 chapters, and the Gospel of Matthew 1068 verses.

No one imagines that this is anything other than sheer coincidence: the Bible was not divided into chapters till the thirteenth century, nor into verses until three hundred years later. But it is a happy parable. Matthew takes up his pen to write up his own abbreviated version of the Hebrew Bible. In our modern translation, his opening words are 'A record of the genealogy ...' But in the Greek in which he wrote, Matthew begins '*Biblos geneseos*', that is 'The Book of Genesis', which is the title of the first book of the Bible.

FIVE VOLUMES

Genesis is only the first of five books which form the bedrock of the Hebrew Bible. Together, this collection of five was known as The Pentateuch, or 'Five Volumes'. So it is interesting that Matthew has divided his Gospel into five as well, and marked the divisions by repeating the same punch line five times: 'When Jesus had finished saying these things' (see 7:28, 11:1, 13:53, 19:1, 26:1). He is quite deliberately writing a new Pentateuch, or *Torah* as the Jews called it, and still do. We usually translate the word *Torah* as 'Law'. More accurately it means 'Teaching'. Matthew's Jesus is no longer simply the Heroic Leader that Mark had wanted to present to the early Christians. He is pre-eminently The Teacher.

ANOTHER MOSES

This of course explains why so many viewers were disturbed by Pasolini's brilliant 1964 film, *The Gospel According to Matthew*. The Jesus the viewers had in mind was a composite figure taken from all four Gospels. Who was this Jesus who never stopped talking, even as he forged ahead down the road with his disciples struggling to keep up with him? The answer is, the Jesus portrayed by Matthew! Pasolini had stuck to his brief meticulously, and presented only the Gospel according to Matthew, of which no less than one third consists of the teaching of Jesus.

Jesus, in fact, is seen as another Moses. He begins his teaching, like Moses on Mount Sinai, with a Sermon on the Mount (5:1). Luke, less interested in this theme, locates the same sermon on a plain (Luke 6:17).

TRUE AND FALSE JEWS

This strong Jewish tone of Matthew derives from the circumstances in which he wrote. In the years 75 to 80AD, two groups of Jews were struggling for survival. One was composed of the shattered remnants of post-war Judaism that had fled to Tel Aviv (Jamnia) on the Palestinian coast, after the Roman destruction of Jerusalem in the year 70. With the Temple gone, and along with it the priesthood, these Jews re-grouped under the leadership of their rabbis, the Pharisees. Modern Judaism is the direct descendant of this group.

The other group was composed of the small band of Jews who had attached themselves to the memory of Jesus of Nazareth. Until recently, they had never distinguished themselves from the first group of Jews. Now they found themselves being ostracized by them, and eventually (85AD) excommunicated as heretics.

Which of the two groups was the legitimate successor of Israel's history? Which were the true Jews, and which the false ones?

FULFILMENT

Matthew's answer is unhesitating. He is quite certain that the Judaism of the rabbis had taken the wrong road by turning in on itself, instead of opening itself to the Roman world, as Christian Judaism had done. The whole direction and purpose of the Hebrew Bible has been fulfilled in the life of Jesus. Matthew uses the formula of 'fulfilment' fourteen times (Luke does so only four times, and Mark only once), and adds a further 150 references to Old Testament texts for good measure. Jesus is the true successor of Moses, and remains the only authoritative teacher. 'He taught with authority, unlike the Scribes and Pharisees' (7:29).

In short, God's own authority has been inherited not by Jamnia but by Jesus, as his final words to his disciples makes clear (28:18). 'God is *with us* (Immanu-El), not with the opposition' is Matthew's statement on his opening page (1:23), and it is corroborated by Jesus on the closing page: 'I am *with you* always, to the very end' (28:20).

Is there an element of anti-Semitism in the stance Matthew has taken? Certainly later anti-Semites have seized on a number of his texts to justify themselves: the frequent ridiculing of Jesus' opponents, the endless 'woes' pronounced against them (chapter 23), their final rejection of Jesus, and willingness to shoulder any responsibility Pilate may have had in the matter, both then and in the future (27:24-25): 'His blood be upon us and our children!'

But anti-Semitism is the wrong word. Matthew was a Semite Jew, as were the readers for whom he was writing. A family quarrel is a quarrel restricted to members of the family, from which we outsiders are asked to keep our distance. Matthew's enthusiasm is that of one who has seen the light, and who is frustrated that his brothers and sisters have not seen it too.

THE CHURCH

In order to give his community of Christian Jews a sure foundation, Matthew provides guidelines, rules and regulations, just as the rival group of Jews were doing at Tel Aviv at the same time. They called themselves 'The Synagogue'. Matthew calls his group 'The Church'. None of the other three Gospels uses this word.

There is therefore a rather churchy and institutional tone about Matthew's Gospel. The Good Shepherd, for example, who in the Gospel of Luke goes in search of those whom society has marginalised (Luke 15:4-7), is presented by Matthew as a concern for Church members who stray from the fold (18:12-18).

With this concern in his mind, Matthew has organised all the teaching of Jesus he can lay his hands on into five great discourses, and so produced a Gospel nearly twice as long as Mark's. He patiently lays down:

> The qualification for membership of the Kingdom
> (the Sermon on the Mount, chapters 5-7)
> A list of instructions for missionaries (chapter 11)
> A series of explanations of the mystery of the Kingdom
> (the Parables, (chapter 13)
> A handbook of Christian conduct, including rules for
> settling Church disputes (chapter 18)
> A description of God's final vindication of the teaching of
> Jesus (chapters 24-25).

REPETITION

This repetitious and meditative approach, again and again starting from the beginning, may pall on some westerners. But it is a tranquil style much appreciated by the easterner, who loves to say the same thing over and over again, each time discovering new riches, and each time getting nearer to the mystery lying at its heart. It is after all the style of nature itself, with its repetitive rhythm of day and night, of new moon and full moon, and of spring, summer, autumn and winter.

The early Church Fathers warmed to the majesty and slow dignity of Matthew's Gospel, and wrote more commentaries on it than on any of the others. Justin Martyr quotes it 170 times, and John Chrysostom bases 90 sermons on it. The Church's liturgy has also shown its appreciation of this majestic style, and until recently chose far more readings from this Gospel than from the others. Matthew's Gospel has in fact been so successful that all Christians know his version of the Lord's Prayer by heart (7:9-13). There are few who could repeat Luke's version (Luke 11:2-4).

ROOTS

Matthew's quarrel with the official Judaism of his time was eventually to cause enormous problems for Christians. But that quarrel is secondary to his main concern – to show Christians how deeply rooted they are in Judaism. If they ever denied those roots, or simply forgot them, they would no longer know who they were: the followers of Jesus the Jew, who never abdicated his Judaism, who advised his followers to forgive endlessly ('seventy times seven') anyone who disagreed with them (see (18:21), and who told them positively even to *love* their enemies if they wanted to remain the children of him whom he called the Father of us all.

'Love your enemies! Yes. I say it again. Love your enemies.
Love – the hardest, toughest, most challenging, most
  invincible force of all.
Love your enemies.
Love those who hate you.
Love those who would destroy you.
Love the man who would kick you and spit at you.
Love the soldier who would drive the sword into your belly.
Love your enemies. We *must* love one another, or we
  must die.'

5:43-48, from Denis Potter's Son of Man

In 13:52, Matthew refers to the teacher, well instructed about the
Kingdom of God, who brings out of his storeroom new treasures as
well as old. It could be a description of himself.

A FEW FOOTNOTES TO MATTHEW'S GOSPEL

1:17 Fourteen generations

Matthew reconstructs a genealogy of Jesus to present him as the descendant not only of Abraham, prototype of all believers, but especially of King David. The Messiah-Christ was looked forward to as another David.

Matthew draws attention to three fourteens in his genealogy. In Hebrew, letters also stand for numbers, and the letters DVD (4+6+4) add up to fourteen. Jesus is the beginning of the fourth fourteen, in other words of the seventh seven. Seven was regarded as the perfect number.

2:1 From the East

Matthew draws attention, from the very beginning, to the universal relevance of Jesus. His birth is good news not only for the 'chosen race', but for outsiders too. Those who imagine they can monopolise Jesus must think again.

3:7 Pharisees

The Pharisees are attacked in all four Gospels, but most strongly in Matthew (see especially chapter 23). This anti-Pharisaism stems more from Matthew than from Jesus. Of course Jesus criticised teachers who were hypocritical or narrow-minded, but then so did the Pharisees themselves. In fact Jesus' teaching in the 30's was in general very close to theirs. It was Matthew, in the 70's, who felt it necessary to assure Jews who had become followers of Jesus that the Pharisaic Jews who had not done so were on the wrong track.

4:17 Kingdom of Heaven

As a devout Jew writing for other Jews, Matthew frequently avoids the word 'God' and substitutes another word like 'heaven'. Even we, heaven help us, still do the same. His phrase 'kingdom of heaven' is exactly equivalent to what the other Gospel writers call the kingdom of God. It refers, not to another world, but to this world once it has accepted and acknowledged the sovereignty of God.

5:20 Law and prophets
Matthew does not want his readers to repudiate their Jewish roots. Like Jesus, they must be even more faithful to the Jewish Bible ('The Law and The Prophets') than anyone else. Matthew does not attack Judaism, but the Pharisaic understanding of it.

7:12 Do unto others
The first century rabbi Hillel was asked how he would sum up the Jewish Bible while standing on one leg. He gave the same advice as Jesus. It's a good litmus test.

8:1 Miracles
Matthew begins the second 'volume' of his Gospel with a series of ten miracle stories. It will end with a discourse (chapter 10) instructing the disciples to go and heal the sick in the same way.

It would be naïve to interpret these miracles as divine proof that Jesus is unique. There have been gifted healers throughout history, among believers and unbelievers alike. The only difference in Jesus' healing ministry is that he saw it as a clear sign that the Kingdom of God was breaking in on the world.

8:20 Son of Man
In the Gospels, Jesus is often said to refer to himself as 'son of man'. Many others did so too, to avoid the word 'I', in something of the same way people refer to themselves as 'one' ('One doesn't like being told to wait'), but without the same affectation.

The first Christians rightly saw possibilities in this, and gave the words capital letters – Son of Man. This could arouse echoes of the weak and suffering Son of Man used throughout the book of Ezekiel (as in this text), and of the glorious and heavenly Son of Man in the vision of Daniel 7.

9:9 Matthew
Mark and Luke also tell this story, giving the detested tax collector the name Levi. Is Matthew humbly coming clean that it was really himself under another name? It was to marginalised people like himself that Jesus proclaimed the good news of God's forgiveness.

10:17 Excommunication
The Gospel again reflects the time in which it was written, rather than the lifetime of Jesus, when the distinction between (Jewish) synagogue and (Christian) church did not yet exist.

12:14 Plot to kill
Whatever could it have been that drove people to kill Jesus? The Gospel pages offer many suggestions: Outrage at his disrespect for sacred institutions? Envy of his popularity? Resentment of his air of authority? Opposition to his liberal ideas? Fear of what they could lead to? Sheer bigotry? Diabolical possession?

Whichever, it was a political charge that finally brought about his death (see chapter 27:11, 29,37,42).

13:3 Parables
Like any good teacher, Jesus did a lot of his teaching through stories. They not only grasp the attention, but deliberately shock the hearers by revealing an aspect of God surprisingly different from what they expect.

15:29 Snap
Like Mark, Matthew tells the story of the Desert Meal twice, with only slight variations. This is presumably how the story stood in their source. Luke and John are bolder, and tell the story only once.

16:17 **The Rock**
Matthew makes much of Peter's profession of faith, which he sees as the foundation stone on which 'The Church' is to be built.

It remains unclear what precise claim is being made here. Is it Peter in person who is the Rock? In which case there is no successor. Or is it Peter's faith on which the Church is built? In which case it is a faith shared by all Christians.

Nor is the Rock as stable as it might be: it can very easily turn into a stumbling block (see verse 23).

18:21 **Endless forgiveness**
Peter's offer is more generous than we realise. He is willing, as few are, to forgive someone for the same fault seven times over. Jesus compares his offer with God's forgiveness, which simply goes on and on. Peter should be glad: he will himself be in need of such endless forgiveness.

22:11 **Wedding clothes**
It is generally agreed that the story of the clean wedding clothes was originally a separate parable, quite distinct from the story of the wedding breakfast, according to which the Good News is on free offer to all outcasts, dressed for the occasion or not. It is Matthew who has turned the two stories into one.

24:3 **Apocalypse**
Matthew, Mark and Luke all conclude Jesus' teaching with an obscure discourse in the style of an 'apocalypse', that is to say, of an 'unveiling' of the future. Though the discourse begins with the forthcoming destruction of Jerusalem (which was the end of *a* world in 70AD), it soon becomes a cosmic prediction of the end of *the* world, when the Son of Man will come to judge us, but no one knows when.

Matthew's practical conclusion is to care for those in need (see 25:31-46), because that is the only criterion we will be judged on. John's Gospel will say the same: the Son of Man comes every day.

27:51 Earthquakes

Matthew alone mentions an earthquake in both the crucifixion and resurrection stories. Since no one else has noted this, it should presumably be taken as poetical language for the 'earthshaking' significance of Jesus' death.

28:6 He has risen

Each Gospel writer tells the resurrection story in his own way, and close comparison can reveal numerous discrepancies. What they all agree on is that the death of Jesus was not the end of him, that his friends experienced him as more alive after his death than before, and that this experience was so real that it changed their lives.

28:19 With you always

Matthew ends his Gospel with a fine sense of rounding off. Jesus preaches his last sermon, like his first, on a mountain in Galilee. The Teacher commissions his followers to become teachers themselves. And the Jesus who embodied the presence of God on page one (1:23) promises to be present with his disciples to the end of time.

The Gospel of
LUKE

The Gospel of Luke – Part 1

Go tell everyone!

ANYONE WANTING TO KNOW what sort of a book Luke's Gospel is should compare the closing lines of his first volume with Mark's:

Mark	Luke
Trembling and bewildered	With great joy
the women went out	the Eleven
and fled from the tomb.	returned to Jerusalem.
They said nothing to anyone	And they stayed in the Temple
because they were afraid.	praising God.

Authors compose their opening and closing lines with great care: they set the tone of the book. Against Mark's background, it was important to stress the fearful responsibility of being a Christian. Luke's background persuaded him to draw attention to the joy to be found in the Gospel, the Good News of Jesus. The words 'joy' and 'praise' occur only once in Mark, and only eleven times in Matthew. Luke uses them 41 times.

THE CHRISTIAN HUMANIST

A comparison of Luke with Matthew is equally enlightening. It has been remarked that turning from Matthew to Luke is like coming out of the church into the market place. There is a feeling of leisurely ease and spaciousness in Luke's Gospel. It is, after all, only the first of two volumes, of which the second ('Acts of the Apostles') will take us into a world the other Gospels don't dream of – from Jerusalem into Samaria, Syria, Turkey and Greece, and eventually to Rome itself, the centre of the civilised world.

So Luke's Gospel is not about dying for your faith (Mark), nor about preserving it behind locked doors (Matthew). It is about living your faith in the ordinary world of men and women. For Luke, Christianity is not a cause for martyrs (Mark), nor a set of regulations for members (Matthew), but a message of common sense for everyone. If Mark can be called the First Christian Dramatist, then Luke is the First Christian Humanist.

ORDERLINESS

Luke's Gospel, like that of Mark and Matthew, was dictated by the circumstances in which he wrote. In Luke's world of 80 to 90AD, the Christian community was expanding rapidly into the Greek-speaking Roman world. This world needed a Gospel attuned to the Greek mind, which demanded not only thoroughness, moderation and universality, but above all order.

For such a world, Mark's Gospel, for all its brilliance, was too haphazard, and its use of Greek almost barbaric. Even Matthew's Gospel, which has its own order of repetition, was too Jewish for the Greek mind. Luke, himself a Greek, and therefore able to write in a style rather kinder to the Greek language, also understood the Greek passion for orderliness.

Look for example at his Infancy Narrative (chapters 1-2), where the first of the prophets Samuel forms a neat diptych with the last of the prophets John the Baptist, so that both can point to Jesus, the fulfilment of all that the prophets ever hoped for.

Look at the way he transfers the daunting genealogy of Jesus down to chapter 3, far more conscious of all his readers than Matthew, who put it on page 1!

Look at his author's preface ('Having checked all the facts with eye-witnesses, I offer this *orderly* account' 1:3) and then assess this statement of intent with chapters 10 – 19 where he has done his own thing and collected vast amount of material not to be found in Mark or Matthew. How reduce this mass of material into some order? By presenting it as one long journey to Jerusalem. Signposts 'To Jerusalem' are planted ten times in this section (9:31, 9:51, 9:53, 13:22, 13:33, 13:34, 17:11, 18:31, 19:11, 19:28), so that the reader will see Jerusalem as not only the starting point but also the finishing point of the Gospel story, which in part 2 (Acts of the Apostles) will spread from Jerusalem to the rest of the world. Greek readers would warm to this sense of orderliness.

SENSE OF PROPORTION

They would also love Luke's sense of proportion. The Greek mind did not like extremes, and would have been quite unable to cope with, say, the Encyclopaedia Britannica. Or skyscrapers. 'Moderation in all things' was their ideal.

So, in the Greek Luke, the mind-blowing mystery of Mark becomes a much more leisurely and urbane story of a good man who went about doing good. The Jesus who spoke from mountain tops in Matthew is here more usually found chatting with friends at table – with Levi over a meal, with Martha and Mary, with Simon at supper, with the disciples at Emmaus. The disciples are no longer reproached for their stupidity: Luke simply leaves the comment out. Or happily changes it: 'Have you got no faith *at all*?' Jesus asks in Mark 4:40. In Luke 8:25 he says '*Where* is your faith? Come on lads!' What Jesus displays, and demands of others, is no longer divine perfection (Matthew 5:48), but simply endless compassion ('Be merciful': Luke 6:36).

Even Jesus' final shocking cry of dereliction ('My God, my God, why have you forsaken me?') is toned down to the much calmer 'Father, into your hands I commit my spirit' (23:46). There is a sense of composure, of soberness, of cooling down and of rounding off the rough edges, in order to commend this Gospel to the civilised Greek world. Dante describes Luke as *scriba mansuetudinis Christi*, the writer who reveals to us the gentleness of Christ.

OPENNESS

The Greek mind was especially opposed to parochialism and narrow- mindedness. Its views were worldwide. Luke, being a Greek, shares these views. And so when he tells us the genealogy of Jesus, he traces it back not simply to the Hebrew Abraham, as Matthew did, but way back to Adam, the forefather of the whole human race (3:38). Nor does Jesus here restrict his ministry to the Jews, as he does in Matthew's Gospel; he goes into foreign Samaritan territory (9:52). He even happily tells a story about a foreign heretic (the Good Samaritan) showing far more practical charity than the Jewish clergy passing by nervously on the other side of the road, just as you or I might do (10:30-37).

This openness to the whole world, not only to your own set, comes across most strongly in Luke's treatment of women and sinners. I'm sorry to bracket them together, but that is exactly what the ancient world did. Both were reckoned to be second-class, and marginalised.

To take the women first. If you had read only the Gospels of Matthew and Mark, you'd hardly be aware that Jesus had any contact with women at all. It's only in Luke that you come across Elizabeth, mother of John the Baptist in chapter 1; of Anna the prophetess in chapter 2; of the widow of Nain whose boy had died in chapter 7; of the female entourage that accompanied Jesus on his missionary journeys in chapter 8 (they're named: Mary, Joanna, Suzanna and several others); of the sisters of Lazarus, Martha and Mary in chapter 10; of the old crippled and bent woman in chapter 13; of the distraught housewife in chapter 15. Most surprising of all, if it wasn't for Luke, we would be almost totally ignorant of Mary the mother of Jesus. She has no speaking part in Matthew, and no part at all in Mark. It is Luke who devotes the whole of his first two chapters to her. It's as if he is the only one of the first three Gospel writers who is aware that the Good News concerns women as well as men.

THE LEAST AND LOST

And then there are sinners and the poor, the least and the lost. They were very easily lumped together in Luke's time. If you were poor, it was because you had sinned. If you were a sinner, you would finish up impoverished. In either case, you were really outside the fold, with no chance of getting a look in. But Luke insists that it is these as well (in fact, these above all) who are the beneficiaries of the Gospel, and have a claim to God's Kingdom. Luke's Jesus is himself born in poverty (not in a cosy cot) as a homeless refugee. The people who witness this birth are not royalty from Persia, but shepherds, the outcasts of Jewish society. (2:7). Luke alone writes up the story of the prostitute who washed the feet of Jesus (7:36-50), of the extortionate taxman Zacchaeus to whom he went for a meal (19:5), of the two criminals in whose company he died (23:39-43). Luke alone tells us Jesus' parables of the Lost Sheep (15:4), and the Lost Coin (15:8), and the Lost Son – about which an Arab bishop once assured me that no Arab father would dare act so extravagantly towards a wastrel son (15:11-32).

It is again Luke alone who tells us the provocative parable of the Publican and the Pharisee (18:9-14). What does it mean to say that an outcast collaborator and extortioner can be closer to God's heart than the most pious religious people of the country? Luke's first Beatitude is not *Blessed are the poor in spirit*, but 'Blessed are the poor full stop' (6:20). It's the have-nots who are the lucky ones. Luke devotes the whole of chapter 16 to the praise of poverty, and draws attention to the danger of money 21 times. (Mark does that too, but only five times. Matthew only once).

For Luke, the Gospel is the Good News for everyone, for all the sons and daughters of Adam and Eve, Gentiles as well as Jews, heretics as well as the orthodox, women as well as men, the poor as well as the affluent – in fact the poor most of all, because they know nothing stands between them and God.

JOY

The joy that shines out of this gospel, therefore, is no afterthought. It is Luke's trademark. Mark had underlined the awesome 'fear' inspired by Jesus. Luke regularly either changes the word into 'joy', or adds the refrain, 'Don't be afraid'. For he sees the story of Jesus as the 'good news of great joy for all people' (2:10). And that is the theme of the first sermon that Jesus preached, according to Luke:

> God's Spirit is in my heart,
> he's called me and set me apart.
> This is what I have to do:
> He's sent me to give the good news to the poor,
> tell prisoners that they are prisoners no more,
> tell blind people that they can see,
> and set the downtrodden free,
> and go tell everyone
> the news that the Kingdom of God has come (4:16-19).

When this Good News was first preached to the crowds by Jesus' first disciples, their joy could even be mistaken for drunkenness (Acts 2:13).

A FEW FOOTNOTES TO LUKE'S GOSPEL
– Part 1 –

1:31 Jesus
For easterners, names are not simply labels: they speak volumes. The name 'Jesus' means 'God has come to save us.'

1:46 Magnificat
In plainchant or polyphony, the *Magnificat* can prove a comfortable and soothing background. In the raw, it is a revolutionary statement close to Luke's heart: God has made a preferential option for the humble and the hungry.

2:8 Outcasts
Matthew tells of the infant Jesus respectfully visited by Wise Men from the east. In Luke they become shepherds, the outcasts of Jewish society. Luke again underlines his interest in the poor.

4:18 Go tell everyone
As Luke tells it, Jesus publishes his Manifesto the first time he preaches in public. Like his mother's *Magnificat*, it is addressed to the poor, the oppressed and the insignificant. They will be the first to recognise his Gospel as good news.

6:12 Jesus and prayer
More than the other Gospel writers, Luke presents Jesus as a man of prayer. At all the key moments of his life (3:21, 5:16, 6:12, 9:18, 9:28, 11:1, 22:32, 22:41ff, 23:46) he turns to his Father in prayer. *The Acts of the Apostles* tell how well his first disciples had picked up the habit.

6:27 Love your enemies
In a country under occupation by enemy troops, Jesus' command to love enemies must have come as a great shock. Yet the God whom Jesus

knew was totally undiscriminating in his love. His Kingdom cannot be established without a similar compassion by everyone for everyone.

8:11 The Prodigal Sower
The explanation of this parable given by the Gospel writers has a pessimistic flavour, as if only a quarter of what is sown bears fruit. Yet Jesus' own telling of it must have been much more optimistic, as sowing is in real life. The incidental losses a farmer sustains in sowing are more than compensated for by the abundant harvest. If they weren't, all farmers would stop sowing. Nor is this simply a lesson in perseverance. The seed is the word which God has always sown prodigally. Hence its unending success.

9:10 The desert meal
Whether it happened twice or only once, what is the reality behind the feeding of the thousands? Was it really a case of magical multiplication? Or did Jesus have a store of bread secretly available in the desert? Or were people shamed into sharing the sandwiches they had brought, so that there was enough for everyone? Or did Jesus literally break each loaf into a thousand pieces, as one would at Communion, and in the circumstances everyone felt satisfied?

The truth is that the evidence we possess no longer allows us to tell. Except that no one would tell such a story of someone unable to satisfy the hunger of thousands.

9:29 Transfiguration
Jesus is bathed in a sort of Easter light in this remarkable experience on the mountain. Luke's observation, that it happened to Jesus 'as he was praying', almost suggests that it could happen to anyone else who prayed.

9:51 Liberation in Jerusalem

Jesus' mystical experience on the mountain, according to Luke, had been a meditation on his departure (Greek *exodos*) in Jerusalem (9:31). What would happen to him there would bring about another liberation of God's people. Hence his resolute journey. The theme is continued by Luke, with repeated reminders, over the next ten chapters.

10:25 Taboos

Luke's parable, read superficially, is a simple lesson in neighbourliness. But to teach such a lesson, Jesus did not need a priest or a Levite, less still a despised Samaritan heretic. His point is that neighbourly love is more likely to arise from ordinary secular human feelings, than from people imprisoned in religious taboos (touching dead bodies made you ritually impure). What religious taboos do followers of Jesus need to break?

10:42 Self-pity

People feel sorry for Martha: she was after all providing the supper. But Jesus' remark is probably only a bit of gentle teasing. She had prepared many 'things' (courses), when Jesus would have been quite happy with one. Why doesn't she stop and come and join in the conversation, which is the best course of all! Her admirable unselfishness could be ruined by self-pity.

12:49 The Peace of Christ

There is peace and peace. The peace that simply bottles up the underlying turmoil is useless. The turmoil will eventually have to be dealt with, even if it means trouble. Christianity is not about being nice to others. To live like Jesus is to ask for trouble. To insist that peace should be built on genuine justice is to ask for a baptism of fire.

14:26 Priorities

Luke, out of character, has failed to translate his eastern source into western language. The easterner tends to speak in black and white, and will say, 'I like this and hate that', where the westerner would say, 'I like this more that that'. Even so, Jesus' demand is costly: discipleship must take priority over everything, even family ties.

15:1 Counterbalance

The three stories in chapter 15 celebrate the endless and unconditional love of God. They are only to be found in Luke, and act as a counterbalance to the more severe stories in chapter 14, also only in Luke.

22:27 Jesus the Servant

Mark and Matthew had placed these sayings of Jesus earlier in their story. Luke puts them here because he finds them more appropriate in the context of the Christian Eucharist. John will later even omit all mention of the bread and wine at the Last Supper, in order to focus on Jesus as the footwashing servant.

23:34 Father, forgive

These words of Jesus on the cross are to be found only in Luke. So also his words to the terrorist crucified with him (verse 43). Luke presents the dying Jesus as a window into the God who puts no limits on his forgiveness.

24:31 The Breaking of Bread

Of all the resurrection stories, this one has always been recognised as the most sensitive, with its blend of the mysterious and the ordinary, of the unknown and the familiar, of darkness giving way to light, and light to darkness. Luke eloquently evokes the Christian Breaking of Bread, where meditation on the Scriptures leads to a recognition of the risen Christ, who is both palpably present, and strangely transient.

The Gospel of Luke
– Part 2 (The Acts of the Apostles)

Jesus continues to be present in the community

I HAVE MENTIONED EARLIER (p.33) that the book to which we have given the title *The Acts of the Apostles* was originally simply part 2 of the Gospel of Luke. Both parts are dedicated to the same Theophilus (Luke 1:3, Acts 1:1), and the second is neatly dovetailed into the first by making its opening lines (Acts 1:1-12) a résumé of part 1.

The two parts became separated early in the second century, when Christians wanted the four Gospels of Matthew, Mark, Luke and John in a single volume, as they now stand in our Bibles. This left 'Luke Part 2' out on a limb, and it was pushed in hopefully between the four Gospels and the collection of Paul's Epistles, under the title of 'Acts of the Apostles'.

But Luke did not choose that title. He is not here trying to write a history (as his contemporaries had done in, say, *The Acts of Alexander the Great* or *The Acts of Hannibal*). He is continuing to write a Gospel. The Good News of what God had done in the life of Jesus (part 1) continues in this account of what God is still doing through the Spirit of Jesus (part 2). This is not a mere chronicle of *how*, but a proclamation *that*. Like part 1, this is not a record written to inform readers about events, but a proclamation inviting their commitment.

In short, unlike the other Gospel writers, Luke wants to make it clear that the story of Jesus is not complete with the telling of his life and

death. You need to tell of his community which spread his message
(indeed his presence) to the rest of the world.

THE BODY OF CHRIST

So it's interesting that Luke (that orderly and methodical and artis-
tic writer) finds constant echoes of the life of the earthly Jesus in the
life and progress of this ever expanding Body of Christ, which is the
Church.

The birth of Jesus in Bethlehem obviously takes place in the presence
of his mother Mary (Luke 2:7). And so she is there also at the birth
of the Church at Pentecost in Acts 1:14. The Spirit of God which
descended on Jesus at his baptism (Luke 3:22) descends on the
whole community in Acts 2:1-4.

When Luke describes the growth of this community, he uses the
same phrase he had used for Jesus: 'In favour with both God and the
people'. (Acts 2:47 = Luke 2:52). Paul sets out on his missionary
journeys in Acts 14:37 with the same text of Isaiah with which Jesus
was first greeted: 'A light to enlighten the Gentiles' (Luke 3:32).

And the book ends, as part 1 did, with a journey up to Jerusalem,
and a trial, and a sentence of death, as Paul becomes another Christ,
as indeed each Christian is called to become.

VIVIDNESS

One of the characteristics of Luke (which makes his Gospel part 1
distinct from the other three) is the vividness of the scenes, which
stay with you long after reading the book. This vividness continues
to be characteristic of part 2 as well.

Think of chapter 2, where the overwhelming joy of the disciples at
Pentecost is mistaken for drunkenness, and Peter says: 'It's only 9.00

in the morning! They're not open yet!' Or of the scene in chapter 3 where a lame man is healed, and he jumps up and down to try out his new feet. Or of the story in chapter 9, where Peter goes down to Haifa to bury an old lady called Dorcas, and the Women's Institute have made a display of all the knitting she'd done for the poor.

Think of chapter 12, where Peter is unexpectedly released from prison, and knocks at a friend's door, and the maid won't let him in, because she can't believe it. Or of chapter 19, where the silversmiths in Ephesus cause a riot because Paul's preaching about Jesus has wrecked their trade in selling statues of the goddess Diana. Poor Diana! Or of Paul's sermon in chapter 20, which goes on so long that someone sitting on the window sill falls asleep and crashes three floors down but survives. His Greek name Eutychus means 'Lucky'.

Think of chapter 26, where Paul is on trial and defending himself, again at great length, and the judge stops him with the words, 'Much more of this, and you'll convert *me* to Christianity!' Or of the scene two chapters further on, where Paul climbs out of his ship-wreck in Malta, only to be bitten by a poisonous snake, and the locals say, 'Obviously a criminal; the gods missed him first time but they've got him now!'; and when Paul shakes it off unharmed, they say, 'Goodness: obviously a god himself!' and kneel down to worship him. Not exactly Music Hall stuff, but there is a great deal of humour there, and lightness of touch, and first class writing, just as in the Gospel.

GOOD NEWS

But I don't want to end this introduction to what we now call the *The Acts of the Apostles* by giving the impression that Luke has written a most readable piece of history. As I said earlier, this book is Gospel, just as part 1 was. And the word Gospel means Good News. And the good news is that the life and activity of Jesus didn't stop when he rose from the dead and ascended into heaven. He continues to be active *in* his community. He and his community are so closely identified that when that community is being persecuted, the voice of Jesus cries out: 'Saul, Saul, why are you persecuting *me*?' (9:4)

Jesus is not dead and gone. He continues to be present in a whole community of people. And this brings overwhelming joy. Luke part 1 stressed this often. Part 2 continues to do so: see 2:46, 5:41, 8:8, 8:39, 13:48, 13:52, 16:34. This does not mean that Christianity is a giggle. To be a follower of Jesus is a stern business. But if it becomes a gloomy business, something's gone wrong.

I draw attention again to one of the opening scenes in Luke part 2. When Jesus' disciples first preached this good news to the crowds, they did it with such enthusiasm that people thought they were drunk. One doesn't hear of many of our clergy being accused of that in these days.

A FEW FOOTNOTES TO LUKE'S GOSPEL
– Part 2 (Acts)

1:8 Summary

This verse forms a neat summary of the ground Luke will be covering in this book. The Good News about Jesus will be spread from Jerusalem (chapters 1-6) into the rest of Judaea and neighbouring Samaria (chapters 7-8), and then under the leadership of Paul (chapter 9) into the non-Jewish world (chapter 10), and the rest of the Roman Empire (chapters 11-28).

1:9 Ascension

To speak of Jesus as 'ascending' is simply to express the belief that he is now with the God who is 'over' the world. But this does not mean that Jesus is absent from the world. He remains present, only in a deeper way. Like Paul, Luke regularly (over 70 times) speaks of this presence in terms of the Spirit of Christ, or the Holy Spirit.

2:1-4 Pentecost

The Pentecost event could be called the Baptism of Jesus' disciples in the Spirit of Christ. From now Jesus is embodied, no longer in six feet of flesh and bones, but in a community.

2:4 Tongues

The phenomenon of *glossolalia* or 'speaking in tongues' is mentioned frequently in the history of religions across the ages. It refers to the ecstatic but unintelligible speech uttered by devotees in a state of high excitement, needing to be interpreted before it can be understood. Presumably this is the meaning of the word here. Luke seems to suggest that the disaster of Babel (see Genesis 11:1-9) has been overcome in an ideal worldwide Christianity, where all people can understand each other again.

2:42-47 Utopia

This vignette of a community at peace with the world and with each other is repeated twice more by Luke, in 4:32-35 and 5:12-16. Was he an idealist, or could this happen again?

5:1-11 Ananias and Sapphira

This story comes immediately before the last of the utopian scenes referred to above, to form a stark contrast. Mr Godgracious and his wife Jewel (this is the meaning of their Hebrew names) cannot fit into a Christian community. This is not because of their wealth (the text insists that it was theirs to keep if they wished) but because of their dishonesty and sham, which made them incompatible with the openness required from those who want to live in the Spirit of Jesus.

8:1 Saul

Notice this tiny vignette painted into the corner of the scene describing Stephen's martyrdom. Luke seems to suggest that the subsequent conversion of Saul (= Paul) begins here. The blood of martyrs is the seedbed from which saints can spring up.

9:1ff Paul

Luke tells the story of Paul's conversion three times (see 22:5ff and 26:1ff). It is as if he can't cease to wonder at the amazing grace that saves wretches.

9:4 The Body of Christ

Jesus, though he has died, lives on in his disciples. They now form the body in which he continues to be present in our world. To touch them is to touch him.

11:28 Luke and Paul

This is the first time that the text uses the first person 'we' instead of the third 'he' or 'they'. It suggests that Luke has joined Paul in his missionary journeys. This usage continues in 16:10ff and 20:5ff (Paul's second and third journeys outside Palestine into Turkey and Greece), and in 27:1ff (Paul's journey as prisoner to Rome).

15:5-35 The 'Council of Jerusalem'

This is the name generally given to the discussion that took place in Jerusalem in the year 48AD on the question of receiving non-Jews into the community of Jesus' disciples. In fact there is evidence in Paul's letters indicating that some of the issues discussed here were not finally settled until years later. Luke seems to have conveniently compressed several years of discussion into a neat single paragraph. For the time being, Gentile Christians were asked to respect Jewish susceptibilities about eating non-kosher meat or food associated with pagan temple practices, and about marriages within certain degrees of kindred. With the decline of Jewish members of the Church, these decrees eventually became irrelevant.

17:23-24 Greek philosophy

Before his first totally non-Jewish audience, Paul decides to preach about Jesus without any reference to his Jewish background. The sermon is an almost complete disaster. Was he right or wrong to refuse ever to do this again (see 2 Corinthians 2:5)?

20:18ff Farewell

Perhaps the most moving of Luke's pages is this last will and testament of his hero Paul. Paul sees trouble ahead, but accepts it as paradoxically implicit in preaching the Good News about Jesus.

27:1ff End of Part Two

Paul makes the final journey of this book, no longer as a missionary but as a prisoner. Yet even here he takes the opportunity to preach the Gospel to his fellow Jews in Rome, the power-house of the Roman Empire. This fulfils the promise with which this book opened, that the Good News about Jesus would be taken 'to the ends of the earth'. Whether Paul was eventually set free from prison to make further journeys (he mentions a projected journey to Spain in his letter to the Romans 15:24) is unclear. So is the theory that Luke (who could have ended the book with Paul's death but doesn't) was planning a Part 3 to tell about the rest of Paul's life and the further growth of Christianity. The last line of Luke's Gospel Part 2 remains as open-ended as the last line of Part 1 (Luke 24:47).

The Gospel of
JOHN

The Gospel of John

Jesus says, God is love, so go and be like him

IN A PARADOXICAL WAY, John's Gospel is at once the easiest and the most difficult of all the four Gospels. Here are two descriptions of the book:

> To take up the Gospel of John after reading Matthew, Mark and Luke, is rather like finding oneself in outer space, when one had merely booked from Paddington to Charing Cross.

Rather disconcerting for the commuter, but for those keen on space travel, what a bonus!

> What first were guessed as points, I now knew stars,
> and named them in the Gospel I have writ.

The death of John in Robert Browning's A Death in the Desert

That is to say, if you want only the 'points' about Jesus' life, go elsewhere – say a *Life of Jesus* such as any Roman historian could have written, or thousands since. John has realised that these points were really *stars*, and does not hesitate to name them and make them explicit, and take you with him to explore them. And if this worries anyone (because they'd really only booked for Charing Cross), they should realise that Mark, Matthew and Luke were also trying to explore space like John, only they don't make it so obvious. At first sight, they look like straight biographies, but they're really theologising quite as hard as John, as we have seen.

THE THEOLOGIAN

The thing about John is that he makes no bones about it. He's quite obviously doing something other than biography. He's explicitly adding his own comments and reflections. You don't have to ask, 'I wonder what kind of theology he's pushing'. He tells you. He spells it out for you a hundred times over. His burial place in Turkey is still called Ayassolouk, a bowdlerisation of the Greek *Agios Theologos* or The Holy Theologian.

It is this, of course, that really makes John far easier to read than Mark, Matthew and Luke. He gives us an explicit interpretation of Jesus of Nazareth, not a hidden one. And because he's so explicit, we've agreed to pay to go on his space-ship, knowing quite well where he's going to take us.

Of all the four Gospel writers, John is the eagle, the high flyer, surveying the scene from a position where he can see the thing as a whole, not in bits and pieces. His view is a global one, an overall view. He stands sufficiently far away (it is thought about 100AD) to have been able to reflect deeply on what the whole picture means, not just the details. 'What first were guessed as points, I now knew stars, and *named* them.'

AN EXAMPLE

An actual example from John's text may make the point more clearly. One of the first stories he tells about Jesus is as follows:

> On the third day there was a wedding at Cana in Galilee.
> The mother of Jesus was there,
> and Jesus and his disciples had also been invited.
> When they ran out of wine,
> since the wine provided for the wedding was all finished,

the mother of Jesus said to him, 'They have no wine.'
Jesus said, 'Woman, why turn to me? My hour has not
come yet.'
His mother said to the servants, 'Do whatever he tells you.'
There were six stone water jars standing there,
meant for the ablutions that are customary among Jews:
each could hold twenty or thirty gallons.
Jesus said to the servants, 'Fill the jars with water',
and they filled them to the brim.
'Draw some out now', he told them 'and take it to the
steward.'
They did this; the steward tasted the water,
and it had turned to wine.
Having no idea where it came from –
only the servants who had drawn the water knew –
the steward called the bridegroom and said,
'People generally serve the best wine first,
and keep the cheaper sort till the guests have had plenty to
drink;
but you have kept the best wine till now.'
This was the first of the signs given by Jesus:
it was given at Cana in Galilee.
He let his glory be seen, and his disciples believed in him.

2:1-11

Notice what is happening here. At one level, we're standing on *terra* that is very *firma*. The 'third day' is a simple reference back to the previous chapter, which told us what Jesus was doing on day one (verse 19ff), on day two (verse 29), on day three (verse 35), and on day four (verse 43). On the third day after that simply brings us to the end of the week. We are keeping a meticulous diary of the first week of Jesus' ministry. This is confirmed by the specification of where precisely this took place (Cana, five miles from Nazareth, verses 1 and 11), who the main guests were (Mary, Jesus and his disciples, verses 2 and 3), and precisely how much wine was involved (6x 20 = 120 gallons, verse 6). From the care taken to place this story in history, geography and accuracy, one can only conclude that we are dealing with something observable, photographic and factual.

And yet, in spite of this emphasis on the really real, the story keeps on introducing overtones of a completely different kind of reality. Its very opening words 'on the third day' evoke the Easter resurrection, which was expressed in these terms long before John was writing (see Acts 10:40, 1 Corinthians 15:4, etc.) So does the word 'glory' (verse 11), which will dominate John's telling of Jesus' death. Similarly the word 'hour' (verse 4), which will crop up again and again in the text to refer to this event. And why is his mother Mary here referred to as 'Woman' (verse 4), and only ever again as she stands by the cross to witness Jesus' death? In the light of all this, could it be that even the miraculous wine is meant to evoke the Eucharist in which Christians ever since have commemorated Jesus' death and resurrection?

So what has this story been about? A village wedding or Jesus' death and resurrection? Why not both? And why do I say that? Because John will continue to do this 'double-take' in each of the stories that follow. Look out for them.

What a strange way of writing! But at the same time, how powerful! The stories are no longer about who Jesus *was*, but about who Jesus *is* for someone who had known him for a very long time.

THE EASIEST OF THE GOSPELS

I have called John's the easiest of the four Gospels. Not easiest to accept or commit yourself to. But easiest to understand: it's not complex. It's not difficult to state what John the Theologian is trying to say. It could be stated in one line: '*While people may say, God is a hard taskmaster, so watch it, Jesus says, God is love, so go and be like him.*' Hardly a complex statement. You'd think that saying it once was enough. Who could fail to understand it?

John is not so naïve. He realises that the simplest things need repeating and repeating before they register. So he himself repeats this simple statement about fifty times in the dozens of vignettes that occupy his twenty chapters. And at the end of them all he concludes: 'There are many other stories I could have used to illustrate the same theme. They are not recorded in this book, because one has to put a full stop somewhere. But I have recorded these stories so that they may nourish your faith, and so give you life in all its fullness.' In other words: 'One single story would have done. It points to the centre, the heart, the hub. I've given you fifty, in order to make that hub solid. When you've read them all, you should know what the heart of the matter is. Though if you had read only one, and understood that, you could have stopped. You'd have got it' (see 20:30-31 and 21:25).

Why then do I call this Gospel, with its simple one-sentence theology, difficult as well? Perhaps because John thought it worthwhile to open up this theology fifty times over. Perhaps this theology is so rich that it not only allows fifty separate approaches, now from this angle, now from that, but actually needs them. Perhaps it's only when you've gone through all fifty of them that you can begin again at the beginning, and realise how rich they are.

JESUS GIVES HIMSELF AWAY

Given this approach, the Gospel of John is rather different from the other three. To begin with, there is none of the mysterious secrecy which is such a strong feature in Mark, Matthew and Luke. Here Jesus is hailed as Messiah, Son of God, King of Israel and Son of Man in the very first chapter. Each of his miracles is a manifestation of 'The Glory' (that is, of God himself), a word which Mark, Matthew and Luke reserve for the Transfiguration and the End of the World. His preaching is no longer about the future Kingdom being like bread or light or a vine or a shepherd. It is about himself, because it is he himself who is here and now the Bread (6:35ff), the Light (8:12), the Gateway (10:7), the Shepherd (10:11ff), the Resurrection and Life (11:25), the Way (14:6) and the Vine (15:1ff).

A similar observation has to be made about the miracles of Jesus. Mark, Matthew and Luke had sprinkled their pages with these stories in a fairly haphazard manner. John has been most careful to select just seven of them, because he sees them all as 'signs' or symbols of the greatest wonder of all – the death that Jesus will eventually die. Many of them are accompanied by a long discourse (three chapters around the man born blind in chapter 9!) to highlight this hidden meaning.

These discourses form another distinctive feature of John. Apart from the parables of Jesus (of which John records none!), the words of Jesus recorded by Mark are little more than punch lines. Matthew and Luke made a stronger attempt to collect the sayings of Jesus and strung them together in their Sermon on the Mount (or on the Plain). John, in contrast, presents a Jesus who keeps making profoundly theological speeches, which spell out the meaning of his ministry. Nor is it always clear where Jesus' speeches are supposed to end, and where John has taken over.

THE LAST THINGS NOW

The most lasting impression that John's Gospel leaves us is one of urgency. Mark, Matthew and Luke all had an element of this in their call for repentance and decision, because 'the Kingdom is at hand,'

And this was continued in the early preaching of Paul, who expected another coming of Christ 'soon'. But John goes a step further. For him, the crisis is not something that will come soon: it is here and now! Consult a biblical 'concordance' to find the many references to the following key words.

For John, the crucial *Hour* for which everyone is waiting has already struck; it is now. The *Coming* of God in *Glory* has already taken place in the life of Jesus; nothing in the future will eclipse that. God's *Judgment* is not something we await: people pass it on themselves by their response to Jesus. The *Eternal Life* which people hope eventually to enjoy is already being lived by those who see God as Jesus saw him. And the *Resurrection* of the dead takes place here and now, when people live in the Spirit of Jesus.

John's remodelling of traditional teaching about the last things is perhaps best seen in his account of Jesus' last discourse before he died. In Mark, Matthew and Luke, this discourse is about the *Second Coming* of Christ in the future. For John (see chapters 13:33 to 17:26), the coming of Christ has no meaning if it is not understood in the present tense.

In the light of these observations we might even be encouraged to re-think the phrases of the famous Lord's Prayer which Matthew and Luke put on the lips of Jesus. John agrees that we should constantly turn to God in prayer and address him as Our Father. But should we pray that his 'name' (or person) should be glorified when it has already been glorified throughout Jesus' ministry, and especially in his death (12:28)? Should we continue worriedly to ask for our daily bread when Jesus himself is the Bread to satisfy the hunger of all people (6:34)? Should we pray to be delivered from the trials of our world when Jesus himself came into our midst precisely to face them (12:27)? The Gospel of John invites people to do more than learn about the life that Jesus lived; it invites them to live it for themselves.

A FEW FOOTNOTES TO JOHN'S GOSPEL

1:1 Plan
The plan of John's Gospel is simplicity itself. Having announced Jesus as the Life and Light and Glory of God, and illustrated this in his preliminary stories (chapters 1 – 2), he opens up the theme of Life in the section which starts and finishes with Nicodemus (chapters 3 – 7), the theme of Light in chapters 8 – 11, and the theme of Glory in the story of Jesus' passion, death and resurrection (chapters 12 – 20).

1:1-18 Word of God
For John Jesus is, as it were, the one Word which God has always spoken, but which becomes most articulate in this man's life.

1:29 Lamb of God
Another metaphor for Jesus: he is, as it were, the slaughtered lamb which every Easter commemorates the saving of God's people.

1:47 Trickster
The first Israelite in the Bible was the patriarch Jacob, whose name means 'Trickster'. Jesus is chaffing this would-be disciple, but promises him a heaven on earth that the first Jacob could only dream of.

2:4 My Hour
The word should have a capital letter, since John repeats it regularly (see 7:30, 8:20, 12:23, 12:27, 13:1, 17:1) in reference to the death and resurrection of Jesus.

4:5-29 Life-giving Water
Like the story of Cana in chapter 2, this chance encounter is heavy with hidden meaning. It is a preview of the scene with which the Gospel comes to a climax, as the pierced side of the crucified Christ pours out the life-giving water of the Spirit, and washes away the barriers that divide one race and faith from another.

6:16-20 Waters of Death

Like all John's stories, even this little episode is meant to evoke the Easter when (as here) 'the disciples went down in the dark, and Jesus had still not rejoined them across the death-dealing waters. Then suddenly they saw Jesus walking on these waters! They were terrified until he said: 'Don't be afraid, it's me (literally, 'I AM')'.

8:3-11 Trespassers will be forgiven

This charming story, missing from many of the oldest manuscripts of John, is probably (according to most scholars) a misplaced piece of Luke's Gospel.

8:58 I Am

In the Hebrew Bible, this is the very name of God (*Yahweh* = He is). John sees Jesus as such an accurate reflection of God in human terms that he does not hesitate to use language which others can only see as blasphemous.

10:1ff. Shepherd

In a less direct way, even this word is a divine title. Although Israel had its human shepherds (the kings), they were ultimately only stand-ins for the one shepherd of the human flock, the God who is willing to give his life to protect them.

13:1ff. Footwashing

It is interesting that, at this point in the story, Mark, Matthew and Luke each tell of the institution of the Eucharist. John replaces it with this story of a Jesus who acts as a humble servant to his disciples, and tells them that this is what they should do in memory of him. It is, of course, rather more demanding than simply going to Communion.

14:16ff. Defender

The Holy Spirit, here referred to as 'Paraclete' (Greek) or 'Advocate' (Latin), is often thought of as some ghostly 'Third Person' who replaces Jesus after he has gone. This chapter makes it clear that this is not John's meaning. The coming of the Spirit is nothing other than the *return* of Jesus to continue his work as 'Defender' of his disciples, that is, to be the very soul of his risen body, which is the Church.

17:16 The World

John's Gospel uses the word 'world' in two quite different senses. At times (as here) it means all that is totally opposed to God. But at other times it means all that God so loves that he sent his only son to save it (see, for instance 3:16). We do well to be wary of the first. We do wrong to despise the second.

20:29 Believing is seeing

Why should John say that believing is more worthwhile than seeing? Surely it's the other way round? Yes, but only in this dramatised story. In actual reality, no one can make contact with the risen Christ unless he believes that Jesus is alive.

Postscript

I THOUGHT IT MIGHT BE USEFUL, in this postscript, to come back again to what is known as the 'Literary Form' of the Gospels. I have not used this technical term in my text, but it has been my subtext throughout.

Literary Forms are to a piece of writing what a Key Signature is to a piece of music. Get it right, and your rendering of the piece will sound something like the composer intended. Disregard it, or worse, get it wrong, and it will sound like bagpipes. A piece of music written in five sharps will kill anyone at five paces if it's played in five flats.

There was a time when the Gospels were presumed to be written in the Literary Form of straight biography, giving us a blow by blow account of what Jesus did and said from day to day. Today the experts are saying that such a view was not only naïve, but disrespectful of the Gospels. They are far more serious documents than that. They were written in a totally different Literary Form. They are a proclamation of the faith of the early Christian community. They offer to tell the reader not simply who Jesus *was*, but who he *is* for a believer. They portray Jesus not as any historian could have presented him, but in depth, as a disciple sees him, in glory.

The disciples do not claim to present simply the kind of Jesus that any Tom, Dick or Herod could have seen, but the much deeper truth about him that his followers claim to have seen. What a Gospel says is: 'For me, Jesus is someone who can walk on the waters of death and not be sucked under. He is the one who enables me to do the same. Does he mean that for you too?'

To put it in a nutshell, we used to read these stories as if they told us about events which could have been videoed or tape-recorded. We now realise that they are something rather different: they are confessional documents, four distinct attempts to express what Jesus means to a believer. Or (to change the image) it could be said that we used to treat the Gospels as if they were grapes to be eaten. In fact they are wine to be drunk, far more nourishing and far headier. The wine is made from real grapes – there are clearly real historical facts underlying the Gospel stories. But it is impossible to reconstruct the wine back into grapes.

Does this kind of approach to the Gospels make them less challenging or more so? Are these modern scholars trying to water down the Christian message to make it easier to swallow? No. They are trying to remain faithful to the original Christian message of *incarnation*. This message claims that the mysterious God, whom people tend to look for up there, in the beyond, in the distance, is to be found down here, close, in something as ordinary as the life of a man, *in carne*. This takes some believing. Far easier to believe in a supernatural being out there. But to see God present, and at work, and clearly revealed in a human being – is that not a form of atheism? That is precisely the charge made against the first Christians by the Romans!

Christians claim to know what God is like by looking at the man Jesus. Not at something beyond him, or behind him, but only at the man that he was. In an utterly human life, they claim to see, undistorted, the face of God. The astronomer Galileo made the profound observation that the Bible wasn't written to tell us the way the heavens go, but to tell us the way to go to heaven. The same is true of the Gospels of Mark, Matthew, Luke and John. They are not information, but an invitation to get on that road.